Puppy Love

KADIE DOWLING

ISBN: **978-1-7381800-0-4**

DEDICATION

"For the devoted and future puppy owners, whose hearts
welcome the pitter-patter of tiny paws and whose homes
become the center of a furry whirlwind, this dedication
echoes a celebration of the journey you're embarking
upon. May the unconditional love, playful moments, and
cherished memories shared with your loyal companions
illuminate your days and grace your lives with
immeasurable joy, unwavering companionship, and a bond
that grows deeper with each passing tail-wagging moment.
Here's to the adventure of nurturing, learning, and loving
your furry friends through the beautiful chapters of life."

CONTENTS

ACKNOWLEDGMENTS

"It takes a village to raise a happy and healthy pup. To all the experienced trainers, passionate veterinarians, and dedicated breeders whose insights and expertise have contributed immeasurably to this guide, thank you for sharing your knowledge and invaluable experiences. Special gratitude to the tireless advocates and animal welfare organizations for their continuous support in promoting responsible pet ownership and ensuring the well-being of our furry friends. To the countless puppy owners who have generously shared their stories and lessons, thank you for being the real-life inspirations behind this book. Lastly, a heartfelt thanks to all the puppy enthusiasts and readers, whose commitment to learning and caring for these wonderful companions inspires us to continue advocating for the happiness and welfare of our beloved pets."

1 Preparing for Your Pup

Bringing a puppy into your home is an exciting and life-changing experience. However, this step demands thorough preparation to ensure a smooth transition for both the puppy and you. In this chapter, we'll delve into the critical steps that precede bringing your furry friend home.

Selecting the Right Breed

Understanding Your Lifestyle. The first step in choosing the right puppy is to assess your lifestyle. Different breeds have distinct temperaments, exercise needs, grooming requirements, and sizes. Consider factors like energy level, space available, family members, and time you can commit to training and care. For instance, active breeds like Border Collies or German Shepherds may not thrive in smaller living spaces or with owners who can't provide ample exercise.

Researching Breeds. Explore various breeds and their traits. Websites, breed-specific books, or talking to experienced dog owners or breeders can offer valuable insights. Consider the breed's compatibility with your lifestyle and preferences. Some breeds might be better suited for families with children, while others might be more appropriate for individuals living in apartments.

Adopting vs. Buying. Decide whether to adopt a puppy from a shelter or buy from a breeder. Shelters offer a wide variety of dogs, often providing a forever home for animals in need. Meanwhile, reputable breeders ensure proper breeding practices, health checks, and support for the pup's early development.

Puppy-Proofing Your Home

Creating a Safe Environment. Puppies are naturally curious and can get into mischief. Before bringing your puppy home, conduct a thorough safety check of your living space. Ensure hazardous items, like chemicals, small objects, or electrical cords, are out of reach. Block off areas that could be potentially dangerous or sensitive for a new puppy.

Securing the Space. Fencing outdoor areas, blocking access to certain rooms, or using baby gates can help manage your pup's exploration and prevent accidents. Additionally, invest in pet-friendly cleaning supplies to maintain a safe and clean environment.

Choosing Essential Supplies

Basic Necessities. Prepare the essentials before your puppy arrives. These include a suitable bed or crate, food and water bowls, quality dog food appropriate for the puppy's age and breed, collar and leash, identification tags, toys for mental stimulation, grooming tools, and a variety of treats for training.

Consulting with Professionals. Seek advice from a veterinarian or experienced pet store staff to ensure you're purchasing the right supplies. Quality food, in particular, plays a vital role in your puppy's growth and health.

Preparing Emotionally

Understanding the Commitment. Owning a puppy is a significant commitment, often lasting 10-15 years or more. Be mentally prepared for the responsibility that comes with training, feeding, exercising, and providing love and care to your pet.

Family Preparation. Educate and involve all family members in the upcoming addition. Discuss responsibilities, boundaries, and proper interaction with the puppy. Prepare children on how to treat the new pup with respect and care.

Embracing Change. Welcoming a puppy into your home brings change and adjustments. Embrace the inevitable modifications in your routine, social life, and personal space, knowing that the rewards of companionship and love outweigh the adjustments.

Preparing for your puppy is a critical phase that lays the foundation for a strong, lifelong bond. Taking these steps ensures a smooth and welcoming environment for your new furry family member.

2 Bringing Your Puppy Home

Bringing a puppy into your home is an exciting but crucial period, laying the groundwork for a lifelong relationship. These initial days are essential for introducing your new furry companion to their environment, ensuring safety, setting routines, and managing the challenges of separation anxiety.

Introducing Your Puppy to Its New Environment

Arrival Preparation. When bringing your puppy home, remember it might be a stressful experience for the little one. Make the journey as comfortable as possible by using a secure carrier or harness. Upon arrival, introduce your pup to one room at a time to prevent overwhelming them with new surroundings.

Establishing a Safe Space. Create a designated area, such as a cozy bed or a crate, where your puppy can feel secure and comfortable. A quiet and peaceful space allows the puppy to acclimate gradually to their new environment.

Initial Interaction. Once settled, gently introduce family members or other pets in a controlled manner. Avoid overstimulation and give the puppy time to adapt. Allow them to explore at their own pace, while providing reassurance and positive reinforcement.

Creating a Safe Space

Puppy-Proofing. Conduct a thorough safety assessment of your home, ensuring potentially hazardous items are out of reach. Cover electrical outlets, secure loose cables, and remove toxic plants or small objects that your pup might swallow.

Establish Boundaries. Use gates or barriers to limit access to specific areas. This helps in potty training and prevents your pup from entering potentially dangerous spaces.

Supervision and Vigilance. Keep a close eye on your puppy during these initial days, preventing accidents or unwanted behaviours. Be present to guide and redirect their attention when necessary.

Establishing Routines

Feeding and Hygiene Schedule. Set a consistent feeding schedule, providing meals at specific times. This supports your puppy's digestive health and aids in house training. Additionally, establish a grooming routine to accustom your pup to being brushed, bathed, and having their nails trimmed.

Toilet Training. Begin toilet training by taking your puppy outside or to their designated toilet area at regular intervals, after meals, play, or waking up. Use positive reinforcement when they relieve themselves in the correct spot.

Play and Rest Cycles. Balance playtime and rest. Puppies need adequate sleep, so ensure they have a quiet and comfortable place to rest undisturbed.

Handling Initial Separation Anxiety

Gradual Alone Time. Gradually introduce short periods of separation to accustom your puppy to being alone. Start with brief absences and gradually increase the duration to prevent separation anxiety.

Comfort and Reassurance. When leaving the puppy alone, provide comforting items like a piece of clothing with your scent or a toy to ease separation anxiety. Also, avoid making dramatic entries or exits, as these might cause stress.

Positive Association. Encourage positive associations with alone time by providing treats or toys that the puppy enjoys, creating a positive environment when you're not around.

The first days with your puppy are vital in establishing trust, comfort, and routine. Providing a safe and secure environment, setting consistent schedules, and managing separation anxiety are fundamental in nurturing a happy and confident puppy.

3 Feeding and Nutrition

Understanding a puppy's dietary requirements is fundamental to their growth, development, and overall health. This chapter explores the intricacies of a puppy's nutritional needs, aiding in the selection of appropriate food, establishing feeding schedules, managing portion sizes, and addressing common feeding concerns.

Understanding a Puppy's Dietary Needs

Nutritional Requirements. Puppies have specific dietary needs crucial for their growth and development. They require a well-balanced diet consisting of proteins, fats, carbohydrates, vitamins, and minerals. An adequate supply of nutrients supports their bones, muscles, immune system, and overall health.

Different Stages of Growth. A puppy's nutritional requirements change as they grow. In the initial months, they need food that supports rapid growth and development. As they mature, their needs change, and the diet should adapt accordingly.

Choosing the Right Food

Quality Matters. Opt for high-quality puppy food. Consult with a veterinarian or a pet nutritionist to select food suitable for your puppy's breed, size, age, and any specific health considerations. Look for brands that meet Association of American Feed Control Officials (AAFCO) standards.

Wet vs. Dry Food. Both wet and dry food options have their advantages. Dry kibble can assist in dental health, while wet food provides additional hydration. A combination or a rotation of both might suit your puppy's needs.

Avoid Human Food. Refrain from feeding human food to your puppy, as it can lead to nutritional imbalances, obesity, and potential health issues. Certain human foods are toxic to dogs and can be harmful if ingested.

Establishing a Feeding Schedule

Consistent Timing. Set a regular feeding schedule to regulate your puppy's eating habits. Most puppies should be fed 3-4 times a day, depending on their age and breed. The schedule should be maintained consistently to establish a routine.

Avoid Free-Feeding. Avoid leaving food out all day for your puppy to graze on. Scheduled feeding helps in managing their bathroom habits and allows you to monitor their intake.

Managing Portion Sizes

Appropriate Portions. Follow the recommended portions based on your puppy's age, weight, and activity level. Overfeeding can lead to obesity, while underfeeding can result in nutritional deficiencies and stunted growth.

Monitoring Growth. Adjust portion sizes as your puppy grows. Regularly monitor their weight and adjust their food intake accordingly to ensure they're receiving the right amount of food.

Addressing Common Feeding Concerns

Transitioning Foods. When changing your puppy's diet, do so gradually to avoid digestive upsets. Mix the new food with the old, increasing the new food gradually over a week or two.

Food Allergies and Sensitivities. Some puppies might develop allergies or sensitivities to certain ingredients. Watch for signs of itching, gastrointestinal issues, or other unusual behaviour, and consult a veterinarian if concerns arise.

Regularity in Bowel Movements. Healthy feeding habits often lead to regular bowel movements. Inconsistencies or irregularities might indicate a problem, requiring attention and potentially a change in diet.

Feeding and nutrition play a pivotal role in a puppy's development and overall health. Understanding their dietary needs, selecting appropriate food, establishing feeding schedules, managing portions, and addressing feeding concerns are vital steps in ensuring your puppy grows up healthy and strong.

4 Basic Training and Socialization

Training and socialization are essential pillars in shaping a puppy's behaviour, adapting them to the household, teaching foundational commands, facilitating social interaction with other pets and people, and exposing them to diverse environments. This chapter dives into the fundamentals of house training, basic commands, socialization, and acclimating your puppy to new surroundings.

House Training Fundamentals

Establishing Routine. Create a consistent routine for bathroom breaks, feeding times, play, and rest. Take your puppy outside or to their designated toilet area after waking up, after meals, and after playtime, rewarding them for eliminating in the right spot.

Crate Training. Utilize a crate as a valuable tool for house training. Dogs instinctively avoid soiling their sleeping area, making it a useful aid in teaching bladder control. Ensure the crate is appropriately sized, providing enough space for movement but not so large that it allows for a bathroom area.

Positive Reinforcement. Use positive reinforcement techniques, such as treats, praise, and rewards, to encourage good behaviour. Reward your puppy when they successfully follow commands or exhibit desired behaviours, reinforcing their learning.

Teaching Basic Commands

Foundational Commands. Introduce basic commands like "sit," "stay," "come," and "down." Consistency, patience, and positive reinforcement are key to teaching these commands. Keep training sessions short and engaging to maintain the puppy's focus.

Leash Training. Begin leash training by introducing your puppy to a collar and leash. Gradually accustom them to walking on a leash, encouraging good behaviour and providing rewards for walking calmly by your side.

Socialization with People and Other Pets

Exposing to New Experiences. Gradually introduce your puppy to different people, experiences, and environments. Begin with calm and controlled interactions, gradually exposing them to various sounds, sights, and situations.

Interacting with Other Pets. Facilitate positive interactions with other pets, ensuring they are well-supervised and in a controlled environment. Monitor body language and intervene if any signs of stress or discomfort are observed.

Introducing Your Puppy to New Environments

Gradual Exposure. Introduce your puppy to new environments, ensuring a slow and positive transition. Expose them to new places, such as parks, streets, or pet-friendly establishments, allowing them to explore at their own pace while offering reassurance.

Positive Association. Encourage positive experiences in new environments by pairing them with treats, toys, and rewards. Create positive associations, making the new surroundings an enjoyable and safe space for your puppy.

Continuous Training and Socialization. Training and socialization are ongoing processes. Regular practice, exposure to different situations, and consistent reinforcement help your puppy adapt and develop good behaviour.

Overcoming Challenges

Patience and Consistency. Training and socialization might present challenges. Stay patient and consistent, using positive reinforcement techniques to encourage good behaviour.

Professional Training Assistance. Seek guidance from professional dog trainers or behaviourists if you encounter significant challenges or behavioural issues that are difficult to address on your own.

Training and socialization lay the groundwork for a well-behaved and adaptable dog. Consistent training, positive reinforcement, gradual socialization, and acclimation to new environments are vital in shaping your puppy's behaviour and fostering a well-rounded and confident companion.

5 Health and Wellness

Ensuring the health and well-being of your puppy is a crucial aspect of responsible pet ownership. This chapter delves into various components of maintaining your puppy's health, covering vaccinations, regular vet check-ups, common health concerns, grooming essentials, parasite control, and overall well-being.

Vaccinations and Preventive Care

Vaccination Schedule. Understanding your puppy's vaccination schedule is essential for protection against common diseases. Core vaccines like distemper, parvovirus, adenovirus, and rabies are typically recommended, while non-core vaccines might be suggested based on lifestyle and risk factors.

Regular Vet Check-ups. Schedule regular veterinary visits for comprehensive health check-ups and vaccinations. These visits allow the vet to monitor your puppy's growth, discuss any concerns, and ensure they are in good health.

Common Health Concerns

Parasites and Pest Control. Protect your puppy from parasites such as fleas, ticks, worms, and heart-worms. Use preventive medications as recommended by your veterinarian and regularly inspect and groom your puppy for signs of infestation.

Nutritional Health. Ensure your puppy receives a well-balanced diet to support their growth and development. Consult your vet to choose the right food and feeding schedule for your puppy's specific needs.

Dental Care. Introduce good dental hygiene early by brushing your puppy's teeth regularly and providing appropriate dental treats. Dental health is crucial for overall well-being.

Grooming Essentials

Coat Care. Grooming your puppy's coat is essential for maintaining hygiene and overall health. Regular brushing, baths as needed, and trimming nails are part of basic grooming routines.

Ear and Eye Care. Clean your puppy's ears and eyes regularly to prevent infections and maintain good hygiene. Use vet-recommended products and techniques for these areas.

Anal Gland Maintenance. Some puppies might require assistance with anal gland expression. If you notice signs of discomfort or scooting, consult a professional for guidance.

Overall Well-being

Exercise and Mental Stimulation. Regular exercise is essential for your puppy's physical health and mental well-being. Engage in age-appropriate physical activities and provide mental stimulation through interactive toys and training exercises.

Monitoring Behaviour and Signs of Illness. Pay attention to changes in your puppy's behaviour or routine. Signs of illness can manifest through altered eating habits, lethargy, unusual bathroom habits, or other behavioural changes.

Emergency Preparedness. Be prepared for emergencies by having a first-aid kit and being familiar with emergency vet services in your area. Quick action during emergencies can save your puppy's life.

Final Considerations

Insurance and Financial Planning. Consider pet insurance or have a financial plan for unexpected health expenses. This ensures that your puppy receives necessary medical care without financial stress.

Spaying/Neutering. Discuss spaying or neutering options with your vet. This procedure can have health benefits and helps control the pet population.

Regular veterinary care, preventive measures, proper grooming, and a focus on overall well-being are essential in ensuring your puppy leads a healthy and happy life. Stay vigilant, address health concerns promptly, and foster a routine that prioritizes your puppy's well-being.

6 Understanding Your Puppy's Behavior

Understanding your puppy's behaviour is key to building a strong and harmonious bond. This chapter delves into deciphering your puppy's body language, behaviour cues, and addresses common behavioural issues like chewing, biting, and barking.

Body Language and Communication

Reading Body Cues. Learn to interpret your puppy's body language. Ears, tail, posture, and facial expressions provide cues about their mood and feelings. Happy, anxious, excited, or frightened, understanding these cues helps in responding appropriately.

Understanding Vocalization. Barks, whines, growls, and other vocalizations communicate different emotions. Identifying the context and tone of these vocalizations helps in understanding what your puppy is trying to express.

Common Behavioural Issues

Chewing. Puppies explore the world through their mouths, leading to chewing behaviour. Provide appropriate chew toys and redirect their attention when inappropriate chewing occurs. Consistency and positive reinforcement help in curbing this behaviour.

Biting and Mouthing. Puppies use their mouths to play and communicate, but they need to learn bite inhibition. Socialization with other puppies helps, and teaching gentle play through yelping or stopping play when they bite too hard aids in training.

Barking. Barking is a natural way for puppies to communicate, but excessive barking can be a concern. Identifying triggers and redirecting their attention, coupled with positive reinforcement for calm behaviour, helps in managing excessive barking.

Training Techniques

Positive Reinforcement. Reward-based training is highly effective. Use treats, praise, or toys to reinforce good behaviour. This method creates a positive association and encourages desired actions.

Consistency and Patience. Consistency is crucial in training. Set clear rules and boundaries, ensuring everyone in the household follows the same guidelines.

Patience is key; avoid punishment-based training methods that might lead to fear or anxiety.

Addressing Specific Behaviour Issues

Separation Anxiety. Gradually accustom your puppy to being alone. Start with short periods and gradually increase the time apart. Leave comforting items or engage in activities that create positive associations with alone time.

Potty Training Challenges. Consistent schedules, praise, and positive reinforcement are essential for successful potty training. Address accidents calmly and redirect your puppy to the designated bathroom area.

Socialization and Development

Early Socialization. Introduce your puppy to various environments, people, pets, and experiences during their critical socialization period. Controlled and positive interactions shape their behaviour and confidence.

Developmental Stages. Understand the different developmental stages your puppy goes through. Adolescence might bring challenges like increased independence and testing boundaries. Adjust training methods to suit their changing needs.

Seeking Professional Help

Behavioural Consultants and Trainers. Consult professional behaviourists or trainers for expert guidance, especially when facing persistent behavioural issues or challenges that seem difficult to manage.

Understanding your puppy's behaviour is an ongoing process that requires observation, patience, and consistent training. By recognizing their communication cues, addressing common behavioural issues, and employing positive training techniques, you can foster a well-behaved and emotionally balanced companion.

7 Exercise and Play

Exercise and play are crucial components of a puppy's life, contributing to their physical fitness, mental well-being, and overall happiness. This chapter explores the significance of balancing physical activity and mental stimulation for a healthy, happy pup. It delves into suitable exercises, playtime activities, and the importance of keeping your puppy engaged.

The Importance of Exercise

Physical Health. Regular exercise is vital for maintaining your puppy's physical health. It helps in weight management, muscle development, and contributes to overall fitness and agility.

Mental Stimulation. Exercise isn't just about physical activity; it also stimulates your puppy's mind. Mental stimulation is key for a well-rounded and contented pet.

Suitable Exercises for Puppies

Walking and Jogging. Gradually introduce your puppy to short walks and light jogs. Adjust the duration and intensity based on their age and breed. Walking not only provides physical exercise but also allows for mental stimulation through exposure to new environments and smells.

Playtime at Home. Engage in indoor games like tug-of-war, fetch, and hide-and-seek to keep your puppy active and mentally engaged. Utilize interactive toys and puzzles that challenge their problem-solving skills.

Interactive Playtime Activities

Training Sessions. Use play as a part of training sessions to reinforce commands and encourage obedience. Training can be fun and mentally stimulating for your puppy while fostering the bond between you and your pet.

Social Interaction. Organize playdates or interactions with other dogs in controlled settings, helping your puppy learn social skills and proper play behaviour.

Importance of Mental Stimulation

Puzzle Toys and Treat Dispensers. Mental exercise is as important as physical exercise. Use puzzle toys or treat-dispensing toys that challenge your puppy's problem-solving abilities and keep them engaged.

Novel Experiences. Introduce your puppy to new experiences and environments. Take them to pet-friendly stores, parks, or on car rides to expose them to different sights, sounds, and smells.

Age-Appropriate Exercise

Young Puppies. Young puppies require shorter, frequent bursts of activity. Avoid excessive physical strain and jumping to prevent injury to their developing bones and joints.

Adolescent Puppies. Adolescent dogs need more exercise to release pent-up energy. Longer walks, more interactive play, and mental challenges cater to their increased energy levels.

Maintaining Engagement

Rotate Toys and Activities. Rotate toys and activities to prevent boredom. Introduce new toys periodically to keep their interest piqued.

Scheduled Playtime. Set a routine for play and exercise. Consistent schedules help in meeting your puppy's needs and providing them with predictable and enjoyable activities.

Tailoring Exercise to Breed and Individual Needs

Consider Breed Characteristics. Different breeds have varying exercise requirements. Some breeds, like working dogs, may need more intense activities, while others, like toy breeds, might require less.

Understanding Your Puppy's Preferences. Pay attention to what activities your puppy enjoys most. Tailor exercises to suit their interests, whether it's running, fetching, problem-solving, or socializing.

Conclusion

Balancing physical activity and mental stimulation is essential for a happy, healthy, and well-adjusted puppy. Regular exercise, engaging playtime, and mental challenges contribute to their overall well-being, supporting both their physical and emotional health. By providing a diverse range of activities and adjusting to their changing needs, you can ensure a contented and active furry companion.

8 Caring for Specific Breeds

Caring for different dog breeds involves understanding their unique characteristics, requirements, and adapting care to suit their specific needs. This chapter delves into the diversity among breeds, discussing the distinct characteristics of various breeds and tailoring care to accommodate those specific requirements.

Understanding Breed Characteristics

Size and Energy Levels. Consider the size and energy levels of different breeds. Small breeds might need less exercise but more mental stimulation, while high-energy breeds require more physical activity to prevent boredom and destructive behaviours.

Temperament and Behaviour. Different breeds exhibit varying temperaments and behaviours. Some are more sociable and require frequent interaction, while others might be more independent or reserved.

Tailoring Care for Specific Breeds

Toy Breeds (e.g., Chihuahua, Maltese)
  - Toy breeds require gentle handling and care due to their small size and fragility.
  - Their exercise needs are modest, but mental stimulation through play and interactive toys is essential.
  - Dental care is crucial for these breeds due to their susceptibility to dental issues.

Large Breeds (e.g., Great Dane, Labrador Retriever)
  - Large breeds require sufficient exercise to maintain their health and prevent obesity.
  - Monitor their growth and ensure appropriate nutrition to prevent bone and joint issues.
  - Train them in obedience and leash manners from an early age due to their size and strength.

High-Energy Breeds (e.g., Border Collie, Australian Shepherd)
  - High-energy breeds need regular and intense exercise to keep them mentally and physically engaged.
  - Engage them in activities like agility training, herding games, or mentally challenging tasks to prevent boredom.

Working Breeds (e.g., German Shepherd, Siberian Husky)
  - Working breeds excel in tasks and require both physical and mental stimulation.

 - Obedience training and activities that tap into their instincts, like tracking or herding, fulfill their need for a purpose.

Brachycephalic Breeds (e.g., Bulldog, Pug)
 - Brachycephalic breeds have breathing issues due to their shortened snouts.
 - Their exercise should be moderate, and they should be kept cool in hot weather to prevent overheating.

Long-Haired Breeds (e.g., Golden Retriever, Cocker Spaniel)
 - Regular grooming and coat care are essential for long-haired breeds to prevent matting and skin issues.
 - Brushing, bathing, and occasional trimming help maintain their coat in good condition.

Specific Health Concerns and Care

Breed-Specific Health Issues. Certain breeds are predisposed to specific health issues. For example, hip dysplasia in larger breeds, respiratory issues in brachycephalic breeds, or eye problems in some smaller breeds. Regular vet check-ups and preventive care are crucial to address and manage these issues.

Nutrition and Diet. Tailor the diet to suit breed-specific needs. Some breeds might have allergies or sensitivities to certain foods. Consult with a vet to select an appropriate diet that suits the breed's requirements.

Breed-Specific Training Techniques. Different breeds respond differently to training techniques. Some might respond better to positive reinforcement, while others might require more firm guidance. Tailor your training approach to suit the breed's temperament.

Conclusion

Understanding and catering to the unique needs of different breeds is crucial for ensuring the well-being and happiness of your puppy. Recognizing their characteristics, adapting exercise, grooming, training, and health care to suit specific breed requirements creates a harmonious and fulfilling environment for your furry companion. Regular observation, consistent care, and adherence to breed-specific considerations foster a strong and loving bond between you and your puppy.

9 Traveling with Your Puppy

Traveling with your puppy can be an exciting yet challenging experience. Whether it's a short car ride or an extended trip by plane, ensuring your puppy's safety, comfort, and well-being is crucial. This chapter covers tips and guidelines for safe travels with your furry companion in various modes of transportation and managing trips or vacations.

Pre-Travel Preparations

Health and Documentation. Before traveling, ensure your puppy is healthy and up to date with vaccinations. Obtain a health certificate from your veterinarian, and carry necessary documentation, such as proof of vaccinations, in case they're required during travel.

Identification Tags. Make sure your puppy has a collar with identification tags containing your contact information. Consider a microchip for added security, enabling easy tracking if your puppy gets lost during the journey.

Car Travel

Safety Measures. Use a secure and comfortable pet carrier, crate, or safety harness specifically designed for the size of your puppy. This ensures they're restrained and safe during the journey.

Frequent Breaks. Plan for regular stops to allow your puppy to relieve themselves, stretch their legs, and have a drink of water. Bring along familiar toys or blankets to provide comfort during the ride.

Traveling on Public Transport

Check Regulations. Research and adhere to the specific guidelines of the transportation service you're using. Different modes of public transport have varying rules and limitations regarding pets.

Behaviour and Comfort. Ensure your puppy is well-behaved, remains calm, and doesn't disturb other passengers. Use a carrier or leash to keep them secure and comfortable during the journey.

Air Travel

Check Airline Policies. Different airlines have specific regulations regarding pet travel. Understand the airline's rules, restrictions, and requirements for transporting pets, including carrier specifications and necessary documentation.

Pet-Friendly Airlines. Choose pet-friendly airlines with good safety records and policies that align with your puppy's needs. Opt for direct flights to minimize stress and avoid layovers if possible.

Managing Trips and Vacations

Accommodations. Plan and book pet-friendly accommodations in advance. Ensure the place you're staying allows pets and offers necessary facilities to make your puppy comfortable.

Familiar Surroundings. Create a familiar environment for your puppy in a new place by bringing along their bed, toys, food, and water dishes. Stick to their routine as much as possible to reduce stress.

General Tips

Carry Essentials. Pack essential items such as food, water, medications, a first-aid kit, poop bags, grooming supplies, and their favourite toys.

Monitor Comfort and Stress Levels. Watch for signs of stress, anxiety, or discomfort during travel. Take breaks and comfort your puppy as needed to ease their anxiety.

Consult a veterinarian. Before embarking on any long journey or trip, consult your vet for advice on travel preparations and tips specific to your puppy's health needs.

Conclusion

Traveling with your puppy requires planning, patience, and attention to their comfort and safety. By preparing in advance, following transportation regulations, and considering your puppy's needs, you can ensure a smooth and enjoyable travel experience for both you and your furry friend.

10 Growing Together

As your puppy matures, your relationship deepens, and your responsibilities as a pet parent evolve. This chapter reflects on the journey thus far, addressing the changing care needs of your growing puppy and fostering a lifelong bond with your beloved pet.

Evolution of Care Needs

Physical Growth. As your puppy grows, their nutritional needs, exercise requirements, and health care change. Adjust their diet, exercise routines, and veterinary care to accommodate their growth and development.

Mental and Emotional Development. Recognize the evolving mental and emotional needs of your puppy. Engage in activities that challenge and stimulate their mind, ensuring emotional well-being through companionship, socialization, and positive interactions.

Training and Ongoing Education

Continued Training. Keep up with training to reinforce good behaviour and ensure obedience. Regular training sessions maintain mental sharpness and strengthen the bond between you and your puppy.

Specialized Training. Consider specialized training, if needed, based on your puppy's breed characteristics or individual requirements. Advanced training or specific activities can cater to their unique needs.

Adjusting to Changes

Adolescent Stage. Adolescence brings changes in behaviour and energy levels. Adapt to their newfound independence and test boundaries while providing guidance and consistent training.

Health and Wellness Adjustments. Monitor your puppy's health closely. Older puppies might require different health care routines, from dental care to modified exercise regimens.

Nurturing the Bond

Quality Time**: Dedicate regular quality time for bonding activities. Engage in play, walks, training, and even quiet moments to strengthen your connection.

Trust and Understanding. Build trust through consistency, positive reinforcement, and attentive care. Understand your puppy's needs and reactions to foster a deeper understanding.

Long-Term Health and Well-being

Regular Vet Check-ups. Maintain routine vet check-ups and vaccinations to ensure your puppy's long-term health. Discuss age-appropriate health care and preventative measures with your veterinarian.

Nutrition and Exercise. Continue to tailor your puppy's diet and exercise to meet their age and health requirements. Adjust their routine to accommodate changes in energy levels and activity preferences.

Future Considerations

Aging and Senior Care. Prepare for your puppy's transition into their senior years. Adapt their environment, exercise, and health care as they age to ensure their comfort and well-being.

Life Changes and Transitions. Be mindful of life changes and transitions that can affect your puppy, such as moves, family changes, or lifestyle adjustments. Ensure these changes are managed to minimize stress and maintain stability for your pet.

Conclusion

As your puppy grows and matures, your role as a pet parent evolves. Adapting to their changing needs, continuing training and education, nurturing your bond, and planning for their future well-being are integral parts of fostering a lifelong, loving relationship with your cherished companion. Through consistency, understanding, and adapting to their evolving requirements, you can ensure a fulfilling and enduring bond with your beloved pet.

SUMMARY

CERTAINLY! HERE'S A COMPREHENSIVE SUMMARY COVERING VARIOUS ASPECTS OF PREPARING FOR, RAISING, AND CARING FOR A PUPPY:

PREPARING FOR YOUR PUP

BEFORE BRINGING A PUPPY HOME, IT'S CRUCIAL TO PREPARE YOUR LIVING SPACE. THIS INCLUDES PUPPY-PROOFING THE HOUSE, GATHERING NECESSARY SUPPLIES (SUCH AS A CRATE, FOOD, BEDDING, TOYS, LEASH, COLLAR, AND GROOMING TOOLS), AND DECIDING ON A SUITABLE VET FOR YOUR NEW FURRY FAMILY MEMBER. ADDITIONALLY, MENTALLY PREPARING FOR THE COMMITMENT AND RESPONSIBILITIES OF RAISING A PUPPY IS KEY.

BRINGING YOUR PUPPY HOME

WHEN BRINGING YOUR PUPPY HOME, CREATING A SAFE AND COMFORTABLE ENVIRONMENT IS CRUCIAL. INTRODUCE THE PUPPY GRADUALLY TO THEIR NEW SURROUNDINGS, ESTABLISH A ROUTINE, AND PROVIDE PLENTY OF REASSURANCE AND AFFECTION TO HELP THEM ADJUST SMOOTHLY TO THEIR NEW HOME.

FEEDING AND NUTRITION

NUTRITION IS A CORNERSTONE OF A PUPPY'S HEALTH AND DEVELOPMENT. PROVIDING A WELL-BALANCED DIET APPROPRIATE FOR THEIR AGE, SIZE, AND BREED IS ESSENTIAL. CONSULT WITH A VET TO CHOOSE THE RIGHT FOOD AND FEEDING SCHEDULE, ENSURING PROPER NUTRITION FOR THEIR GROWTH.

BASIC TRAINING AND SOCIALIZATION

EARLY TRAINING AND SOCIALIZATION PLAY A VITAL ROLE IN A PUPPY'S DEVELOPMENT. TEACHING BASIC COMMANDS, HOUSE TRAINING, AND INTRODUCING THEM TO VARIOUS ENVIRONMENTS, PEOPLE, AND OTHER ANIMALS HELPS IN SHAPING A WELL-BEHAVED AND WELL-ADJUSTED ADULT DOG.

HEALTH AND WELLNESS

REGULAR VET CHECK-UPS, VACCINATIONS, PARASITE CONTROL, AND PREVENTIVE HEALTHCARE ARE FUNDAMENTAL FOR A PUPPY'S OVERALL WELL-BEING. OBSERVING CHANGES IN BEHAVIOR, MONITORING THEIR WEIGHT, AND STAYING VIGILANT FOR ANY SIGNS OF ILLNESS OR DISCOMFORT IS CRUCIAL FOR THEIR HEALTH.

UNDERSTANDING YOUR PUPPY'S BEHAVIOR

UNDERSTANDING YOUR PUPPY'S BODY LANGUAGE, BEHAVIOR, AND COMMUNICATION CUES IS CRUCIAL FOR EFFECTIVE TRAINING AND A STRONG HUMAN-DOG BOND. RECOGNIZING SIGNS OF STRESS, FEAR, EXCITEMENT, AND CONTENTMENT HELPS IN RESPONDING APPROPRIATELY TO THEIR NEEDS.

EXERCISE AND PLAY

PUPPIES NEED ADEQUATE EXERCISE AND MENTAL STIMULATION TO STAY HEALTHY AND HAPPY. STRUCTURED PLAYTIME AND EXERCISE SESSIONS HELP BURN OFF ENERGY, STIMULATE THEIR MINDS, AND PREVENT BEHAVIORAL ISSUES CAUSED BY BOREDOM OR EXCESS ENERGY.

CARING FOR SPECIFIC BREEDS

DIFFERENT BREEDS HAVE UNIQUE NEEDS AND CHARACTERISTICS. RESEARCH AND UNDERSTAND THE SPECIFIC REQUIREMENTS, TENDENCIES, AND POTENTIAL HEALTH ISSUES ASSOCIATED WITH YOUR PUPPY'S BREED TO PROVIDE TAILORED CARE AND ENSURE THEIR WELL-BEING.

TRAVELING WITH YOUR PUPPY

IF YOU PLAN TO TRAVEL WITH YOUR PUPPY, WHETHER ON SHORT TRIPS OR LONGER JOURNEYS, IT'S IMPORTANT TO PREPARE THEM FOR TRAVEL AND ENSURE THEIR COMFORT AND SAFETY. THIS INCLUDES CRATE TRAINING, NECESSARY DOCUMENTS, TRAVEL ESSENTIALS, AND ACCLIMATIZATION TO CAR RIDES.

GROWING TOGETHER

AS YOUR PUPPY GROWS INTO AN ADULT DOG, YOUR RELATIONSHIP WILL CONTINUE TO EVOLVE. BEING PATIENT, CONSISTENT, AND MAINTAINING TRAINING AND CARE ROUTINES WILL STRENGTHEN THE BOND BETWEEN YOU AND YOUR FURRY COMPANION.

THIS COMPREHENSIVE APPROACH COVERING VARIOUS ASPECTS OF PUPPY CARE AND DEVELOPMENT AIMS TO PROVIDE A SOLID FOUNDATION FOR A FULFILLING AND REWARDING JOURNEY WITH YOUR NEW CANINE FAMILY MEMBER.

ABOUT THE AUTHOR

Kadie Dowling is a seasoned author renowned for her expertise in the realm of canine care, particularly in her dedication to the well-being of dogs. With a wealth of experience with canines Kadie"s writing illuminates her deep understanding of nurturing and training dogs, emphasizing the specific needs and care required for canines. Her insightful and compassionate approach in her works reflects her commitment to ensuring every beloved pet receives the utmost care and attention they deserve.

Important information to keep track of you can save it right here for your records or if you purchased this as an E-Book you have my permission to print yourself a copy.

Pets Name:

Bread:

Date of birth:

Does the Puppy have a Microchip?   YES   NO

Important Information

Certainly! Keeping detailed records about your puppy is essential for their health and well-being. Here's an outline of the kind of records you should maintain:

1. Health Records
a. Vaccination and Medical History.
Document all vaccinations, including dates, types, and boosters administered. Also, record any medical treatments or procedures undergone.
b. Medication Log. Keep a log of any prescribed medications, dosages, and administration schedules.

Vet Check List

- [ ] Filled-out forms provided by your vet
- [ ] All veterinary records you received from the shelter/rescue/breeder
- [ ] List of important questions or concerns you may have
- [ ] Notes on amount and brand of food and treats you offer at home
- [ ] Any medications you were given by the shelter/rescue/breeder
- [ ] Leash and collar/harness
- [ ] Chew toy for distraction
- [ ] Small treats to reward good behavior
- [ ] A stool sample, as fresh as possible
- [ ] Dog carrier or crate lined with a towel or shirt that smells like home

2. Growth and Development
a. Weight and Growth Chart. Track the puppy's weight changes over time to ensure healthy growth.
b. Milestones and Behavior. Note developmental milestones, such as when they start walking, teething, or achieving training milestones.

_____
_____
_____
_____
_____
_____
_____
_____
_____
_____
_____
_____
_____
_____
_____
_____
_____
_____
_____
_____
_____
_____
_____

3. Feeding and Dietary Records
a. Feeding Schedule. Record the type of food, feeding times, and quantities fed.
b. Food Allergies or Reactions. Document any allergic reactions or digestive issues related to food.

	MORNING	AFTERNOON	NIGHT	TREATS
SUNDAY				
MONDAY				
TUESDAY				
WEDNESDAY				
THURSDAY				
FRIDAY				
SATURDAY				

HOW MUCH SHOULD I FEED MY PUPPY?
It depends on your puppy's **age, weight** (including expected
adult weight) and **body condition score**. Follow the feeding
chart on your brand of puppy food and the advice of your vet.

4. Training and Behavioral Records
a. Training Progress. Note the progress in obedience training, housebreaking, and socialization efforts.
b. Behavioral Notes. Keep a log of any behavior issues, changes, or concerns for future training or behavioral adjustments.

DATE	TIME	PEE	POO	ACCIDENT?	NOTES

Puppy Love

5. Veterinary Visits and Check-ups
a. Appointment Dates. Maintain a record of all vet visits, including routine check-ups and emergency visits.
b. Veterinary Recommendations. Jot down advice or recommendations from the vet for future reference.

6. Parasite Control and Prevention
a. Flea and Tick Prevention. Keep a log of
treatments and their effectiveness.
b. Deworming Schedule. Maintain a record of
deworming treatments and schedules.

7. Environmental and Social Exposure
a. Socialization Experiences. Note any exposure to new environments, people, and other animals.
b. Environmental Changes. Document any major changes in the puppy's living conditions.

_____
_____
_____
_____
_____
_____
_____
_____
_____
_____
_____
_____
_____
_____
_____
_____
_____
_____
_____
_____
_____
_____
_____
_____

8. Medical Emergency Preparedness
a. Emergency Contacts. List emergency vet
contacts and poison control hotlines.
b. First Aid Responses. Document any first aid
administered during emergencies.

9. Behavioral Observations
a. Daily Observations. Maintain a log of daily
behaviors, playtime, and activities.
b. Concerns or Anomalies. Note any unusual
behaviors or health concerns for future reference.

10. Photographic and Video Records

a. Visual Record Keeping: Capture photos and videos of your puppy at different stages for visual reference of their growth and development.

By maintaining these detailed records, you'll be better equipped to track your puppy's health, behaviour, and development, aiding both your vet and you in providing optimal care and training.

Coming Soon!

We have a few addition titles in our Caring About You Dog Series that are almost ready to be released.

You and Your Adult Dog

Chapter 1: Understanding Your Adult Dog

Key Points: Exploring the unique characteristics and needs of adult dogs. Understanding their behavior, body language, and temperament changes from puppyhood.

Chapter 2: Nutrition for Adult Dogs

Key Points: Discussing the specific dietary requirements of adult dogs, selecting appropriate food, portion control, and managing special diets.

Chapter 3: Exercise and Fitness

Key Points: Detailing the importance of exercise for adult dogs, tailored exercise plans for different breeds, and incorporating mental stimulation into their routines.

Chapter 4: Grooming and Hygiene

Key Points: Covering grooming practices, such as bathing, brushing, nail trimming, and specialized care for different coat types. Additionally, addressing dental and ear care.

Chapter 5: Health Care and Veterinary Visits

Key Points: Highlighting the significance of regular vet check-ups, vaccinations, preventive care, signs of health issues, and understanding common ailments in adult dogs.

Chapter 6: Training and Behavioral Development

Key Points: Exploring training methods for obedience, socialization, and addressing specific behavioral issues common in adult dogs.

Chapter 7: Enrichment and Mental Stimulation

Key Points: Discussing the importance of mental stimulation, offering various activities to keep adult dogs mentally engaged, and preventing boredom.

Chapter 8: Understanding Canine Communication

Key Points: Examining dog body language, vocalizations, and communication signals to better understand your adult dog's needs and emotions.

Chapter 9: Managing Changes and Aging

Key Points: Guidance on caring for older adult dogs, addressing their changing needs, health concerns, and adjustments in lifestyle.

Chapter 10: Creating a Holistic Approach to Care

Key Points: Summarizing a holistic approach to adult dog care, combining nutrition, exercise, grooming, health care, and behavior into a comprehensive plan for a happy and healthy adult dog.

Each chapter can encompass detailed information, tips, and insights to help dog owners navigate the various aspects of caring for their adult canine companions. If you want more information on any specific chapter or need to explore a particular area in more depth.

Life With a Senior Dog

Chapter 1: Understanding Your Senior Dog

Key Points: Exploring the changes in behavior, health, and needs of senior dogs, including how to provide the best care during their later years.

Chapter 2: Senior Dog Nutrition and Diet

Key Points: Discussing dietary adjustments, specific nutritional requirements, managing weight, and addressing health conditions through diet for aging dogs.

Chapter 3: Health Care and Common Senior Dog Issues

Key Points: Addressing common health concerns in senior dogs, recognizing signs of aging-related illnesses, and understanding how to manage their health effectively.

Chapter 4: Exercise and Physical Activity for Senior Dogs

Key Points: Tailoring exercise routines, low-impact activities, and mobility exercises to maintain fitness and health for older dogs.

Chapter 5: Grooming and Hygiene for Senior Dogs

Key Points: Detailing special grooming considerations for senior dogs, including dental care, skin, coat, and joint-related grooming practices.

Chapter 6: Environmental Adaptations for Senior Dogs

Key Points: Discussing necessary home modifications, bedding, and environmental adjustments to improve comfort and mobility for senior dogs.

Chapter 7: Behavior and Cognitive Changes in Senior Dogs

Key Points: Addressing cognitive decline, behavioral changes, and methods to enhance mental stimulation for senior dogs.

Chapter 8: Palliative Care and End-of-Life Planning

Key Points: Guidance on end-of-life care, recognizing when a dog is approaching the end of its life, and providing comfort during this stage.

Chapter 9: Emotional Support for Senior Dog Owners

Key Points: Discussing the emotional impact of caring for an aging dog, coping strategies, and seeking support during this phase.

Chapter 10: Celebrating the Senior Dog's Life

Key Points: Focusing on cherishing the time with a senior dog, creating lasting memories, and ensuring their final years are filled with love and joy.

Each chapter aims to provide a comprehensive understanding and specific guidance on caring for a senior dog, considering their unique needs, health concerns, and the special care required during this stage of life.

How To Deal with The Loss of Your Dog

Chapter 1: Understanding Grief and Pet Loss

Key Points: Addressing the emotions and stages of grief experienced when losing a family dog, normalizing feelings of loss, and recognizing the impact of pet bereavement.

Chapter 2: Coping Strategies for Pet Loss

Key Points: Offering coping mechanisms, self-care practices, and strategies to navigate the grieving process and find emotional support during this difficult time.

Chapter 3: Exploring the Human-Animal Bond

Key Points: Celebrating the unique bond between humans and their pets, understanding the depth of the relationship, and honoring the memories shared.

Chapter 4: Supporting Children Through Pet Loss

Key Points: Addressing the impact of pet loss on children, providing guidance on discussing the loss, and helping children cope with their emotions.

Chapter 5: Memorializing and Honoring Your Dog

Key Points: Exploring different ways to create lasting tributes, such as memorials, keepsakes, or rituals, to honor the memory of the departed pet.

Chapter 6: Dealing with Guilt and Regret

Key Points: Discussing feelings of guilt and regret associated with pet loss and providing methods to work through and cope with these emotions.

Chapter 7: The Decision-Making Process: Euthanasia and Quality of Life

Key Points: Offering guidance on the difficult decision of euthanasia, understanding a pet's quality of life, and dealing with the aftermath of the decision.

Chapter 8: Seeking Support and Pet Loss Resources

Key Points: Exploring avenues for support, such as pet loss support groups, counseling services, and online resources for those mourning the loss of a pet.

Chapter 9: Moving Forward and Finding Closure

Key Points: Addressing the process of healing, finding closure, and eventually considering opening your heart to a new pet or finding ways to continue the legacy of your lost pet.

Chapter 10: Creating a Lasting Legacy

Key Points: Discussing ways to honor the memory of the family dog through acts of kindness, charitable donations, or involvement in pet advocacy to create a positive impact in their memory.

These chapters aim to provide guidance, support, and coping strategies for individuals and families navigating the difficult journey of losing a beloved family dog.

Puppy Love